Respecting the Contributions of
LGBT Americans

Anna Kingston

PowerKiDS press™

New York

Published in 2013 by The Rosen Publishing Group, Inc.
29 East 21st Street, New York, NY 10010

First Edition

Editor: Jennifer Way
Book Design: Erica Clendening and Ashley Drago
Layout Design: Andrew Povolny

Photo Credits: Cover, p. 21 Frazer Harrison/Getty Images; p. 5 Orlando Marques/First Light/Getty Images; p. 6 Digital Vision/Thinkstock; p. 7 Taylor Hill/Getty Images; p. 8 Jenkins/Hulton Archive/Getty Images; p. 9 Spencer Platt/Getty Images; p. 10 Fred W. McDarrah/Premium Archive/Getty Images; p. 11 Stan Honda/AFP/Getty Images; p. 12 Associated Press; p. 13 Jemal Countess/Getty Images; p. 14 Dirck Halstead/Time & Life Images/Getty Images; p. 15 Jason Kempin/Getty Images; p. 17 Alex Wong/Getty Images; p. 18 Mario Tama/Getty Images; p. 19 Neilson Barnard/Getty Images; p. 20 Saul Loeb/AFP/Getty Images; p. 22 Bruce Rogovin/Photolibrary/Getty Images.

Library of Congress Cataloging-in-Publication Data

Kingston, Anna.
 Respecting the contributions of LGBT Americans / by Anna Kingston. — 1st ed.
     p. cm. — (Stop bullying now!)
 Includes index.
 ISBN 978-1-4488-7446-0 (library binding) — ISBN 978-1-4488-7519-1 (pbk.) —
ISBN 978-1-4488-7593-1 (6-pack)
 1. Gays—United States—History. 2. Lesbians—United States—History. 3. Equality. I. Title.
 HQ76.3.U5K56 2013
 306.76'6—dc23

                              2012002901

Manufactured in the United States of America

CPSIA Compliance Information: Batch #SW12PK: For Further Information contact Rosen Publishing, New York, New York at 1-800-237-9932

Contents

The idea that all people are equal has been important throughout American history. However, certain groups of Americans have had to fight for their rights over the years. LGBT Americans are still fighting **discrimination** today. "LGBT" is short for "**lesbian, gay, bisexual**, and **transgender**."

Lesbians are women who fall in love with women. Gay men fall in love with other men. People who can fall in love with both men and women are known as bisexual. Transgender people identify with a different gender from the one into which they were born.

Pride marches are held every year in cities around the world. The marches celebrate the LGBT community and the fight for LGBT rights.

▶

What Is Bullying?

Bullies are people who hurt or scare other people. Some bullies beat up kids who are different. Bullying is a problem for many young LGBT Americans and children with LGBT parents.

Spreading rumors and excluding people are two ways bullies hurt people. ▼

Each year, Broadway stars perform in an event for the Trevor Project. This organization helps bullied LGBT youth.

There are other ways bullies can hurt people besides beating them up. Spreading rumors is bullying. Making fun of people is as well. Some bullies make fun of people and spread rumors in person, while others do so online. Bullies also hurt other people by leaving them out. For example, a bully might refuse to be friends with a kid who has gay dads or lesbian moms.

James Baldwin was an African American writer who was gay. In the 1950s, he wrote books with characters who identified as gay. At this time, many people kept the fact that they were gay a secret.

For most of American history, LGBT Americans could not live openly. People risked losing their jobs and being shunned by their families or even being killed for having a gay or lesbian relationship. States even passed laws that sent people to jail for having gay or lesbian relationships. For these reasons, people felt the need to keep the fact that they were gay or lesbian a secret.

Maurice Sendak is the author of the classic children's book *Where the Wild Things Are*. Sendak is gay, but he did not talk about it publicly until late in his life.

In 1961, Illinois became the first state to pass a law saying **homosexuality**, or being gay or lesbian, is not a crime. The last of these laws was not thrown out until 2003.

When people could be thrown into jail for being LGBT, they often went to bars where they knew they could meet other LGBT people. Police sometimes raided those bars and arrested people. People grew tired of hiding their true selves or risking arrest. They decided to fight for their rights.

One month after the Stonewall riots, a rally in support of LGBT rights was held in New York City.

On June 28, 1969, police raided a bar called the Stonewall Inn, in New York City. Some of the people the police tried to arrest started fighting back. LGBT people from the neighborhood joined the protests, too. The Stonewall **riots** are seen as the start of the LGBT rights movement.

Here is the Stonewall Inn today. Each year during the New York City Pride March, people gather outside the bar to celebrate its place in history.

Harvey Milk was a politician and an LGBT rights **activist**. He was born in 1930, in Woodmere, New York. In 1972, he moved to San Francisco, California. He settled in a neighborhood called the Castro that was home to many gay men and became a community leader.

When he was elected, Milk said, "This is not my victory, it's yours. If a gay man can win, it proves that there is hope for all minorities who are willing to fight."

Today, LGBT people serve at all levels of government. Here, New York City Council Speaker Christine Quinn (center), who is a lesbian, takes part in the city's 2011 Pride March.

In 1977, Milk was elected to the San Francisco County Board of Supervisors. He became America's first openly gay elected official. Sadly, a man who was against LGBT rights killed Milk in 1978. Milk paved the way for greater acceptance of openly LGBT politicians, who today serve as leaders in local, state, and national governments.

In the early 1980s, gay men across the United States started dying from a mysterious sickness. In 1982, doctors named the sickness **AIDS**. The number of people dying of AIDS kept growing. However,

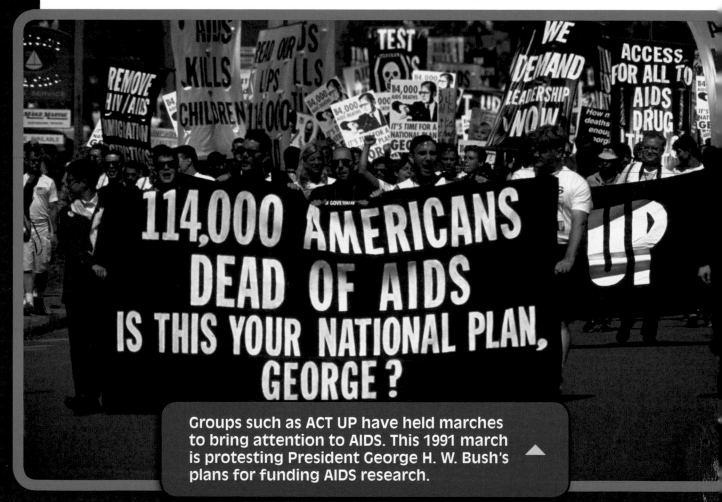

Groups such as ACT UP have held marches to bring attention to AIDS. This 1991 march is protesting President George H. W. Bush's plans for funding AIDS research.

the government paid little attention. This likely happened because many people were **prejudiced** against the gay men who were the main group dying of AIDS at this time.

The LGBT community came together to raise awareness about and fight AIDS. Groups formed to care for people with AIDS and educate others about it. In 1987, activist Cleve Jones helped organize the AIDS Memorial Quilt to honor those who had died of AIDS.

Larry Kramer (1935-)

Larry Kramer is a writer and LGBT rights activist. His 1985 play *The Normal Heart* brought attention to the AIDS crisis. He helped start the Gay Men's Health Crisis, which cares for people with AIDS. He also founded ACT UP, an AIDS awareness group that promotes funding for AIDS research.

Until recently, LGBT Americans could not serve openly in the US military. In 1993, the military started following a policy, or rule, called "don't ask, don't tell." It said that people in the military could not be asked if they were LGBT. It also meant that people in the military could not tell anyone if they were LGBT.

Members of the military who were dismissed for being LGBT spoke out against the policy. On December 18, 2010, Congress voted to end "don't ask, don't tell." The policy officially ended on September 20, 2011.

These people were calling for the repeal of "don't ask, don't tell" shortly before Congress voted to end it. It is estimated that 13,000 soldiers were dismissed under this policy.

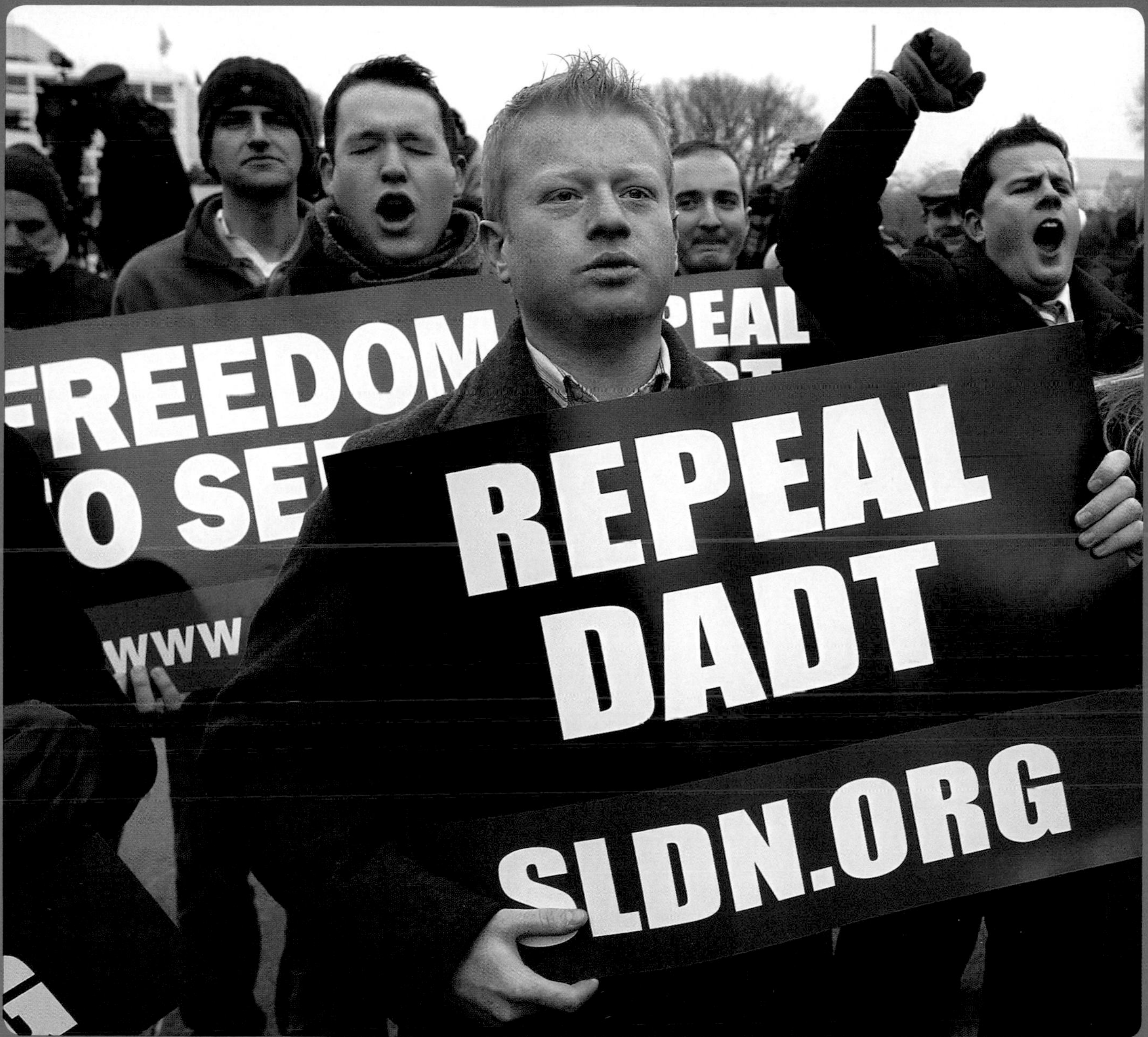
FREEDOM
O SE
WWW
REPEAL
DADT
SLDN.ORG

Marriage equality became the law in New York in 2011. Many couples waited in line for hours to marry on the day it became legal.

The Right to Say "I Do"

One thing that LGBT Americans are fighting for is **marriage equality**. For hundreds of years, gay men and lesbians have not been able to marry the people they love. Being married makes things like visiting the person you love in the hospital easier.

Marriage equality still does not exist in most US states. However, people across the country are working to change this. In 2004, Massachusetts became the first state to allow gay men and lesbians to marry. Since that time, marriage equality has come to other states, such as New York, Iowa, and Connecticut.

Chaz Bono (1969–)

Chaz Bono is an LGBT activist who is the child of Sonny Bono and Cher. Bono was born a female and named Chastity. Over time, Bono came out as transgender and went through a **gender transition** to become a male. He wrote a book to help others understand his story.

The families of Matthew Shepard and James Byrd Jr. met with President Barack Obama in 2009 when the Matthew Shepard and James Byrd, Jr. Hate Crimes Prevention Act was signed.

Some people's prejudice against LGBT Americans is so strong that they do horrible things to them. Sadly, attacks on LGBT Americans are becoming more common.

In 2009, the Matthew Shepard and James Byrd, Jr. Hate Crimes Prevention Act was signed. Part of this federal law makes attacking LGBT people a hate crime. This means it is considered a very serious crime. The act was named in part for Matthew Shepard. He was a gay man who died after he was beaten in Laramie, Wyoming, in 1998. His parents started a foundation, which tries to "replace hate with understanding, **compassion**, and acceptance."

Ellen DeGeneres (1958–)

In 1997, Ellen DeGeneres became among the first famous people to come out as a lesbian. Since 2003, she has hosted a popular, Emmy-winning talk show. DeGeneres uses her popularity to speak out on important issues, such as for marriage equality and against the bullying of LGBT teens.

Respecting Everybody

Today, LGBT Americans are more likely to come out, or say that they are lesbian, gay, bisexual, or transgender. There are many famous LGBT Americans. The writer Alice Walker is bisexual, while actors Chris Colfer and Neil Patrick Harris are gay.

However, bullying remains a problem for LGBT kids. We can all help, though. Remind others that "gay" is not an insult. Stick up for LGBT people who are being bullied. Remember, everyone deserves respect!

Learning to respect the different kinds of people who make up America helps you understand the struggles different groups have faced.

Glossary

activist (AK-tih-vist) Someone who takes action for what he or she believes is right.

AIDS (AYDZ) An illness of the immune system.

bisexual (by-SEK-shuh-wul) Someone who can fall in love with both men and women.

compassion (kum-PA-shin) Kindness.

discrimination (dis-krih-muh-NAY-shun) Treating a person badly or unfairly just because he or she is different.

gay (GAY) Someone who falls in love with someone of the same gender.

gender transition (JEN-der trants-SIH-shun) When people take steps to change their gender from their birth gender to the one that they feel themselves to be.

homosexuality (hoh-muh-sek-shuh-WA-luh-tee) Falling in love with people of the same gender.

lesbian (LEZ-bee-un) A woman who falls in love with other women.

marriage equality (MER-ij ih-KWAH-luh-tee) The right of all people to marry the person of their choosing no matter their gender.

prejudiced (PREH-juh-disd) Disliked a group of people different from you.

riots (RY-uts) Groups of people that are disorderly and out of control.

transgender (trants-JEN-der) People who identify personally as being a different gender from the one into which they were born.

Index

Websites

Due to the changing nature of Internet links, PowerKids Press has developed an online list of websites related to the subject of this book. This site is updated regularly. Please use this link to access the list:
www.powerkidslinks.com/sbn/lgbt/